THREE THIEVES
BOOK FOUR

The King's Dragon

Kids Can Press acknowledges the financial support of the Government of Ontario, through the Ontario Media Development Corporation's Ontario Book Initiative; the Ontario Arts Council; the Canada Council for the Arts; and the Government of Canada, through the CBF, for our publishing activity.

Published in Canada by
Kids Can Press Ltd.
25 Dockside Drive
Toronto, ON M5A 0B5

Published in the U.S. by
Kids Can Press Ltd.
2250 Military Road
Tonawanda, NY 14150

www.kidscanpress.com

Edited by Karen Li and Yasemin Uçar
Designed by Scott Chantler and Marie Bartholomew
Pages lettered with Blambot comic fonts

The hardcover edition of this book is smyth sewn casebound.
The paperback edition of this book is limp sewn with a drawn-on cover.
Manufactured in Buji, Shenzhen, China, in 11/2013 by WKT Company

CM 14 0 9 8 7 6 5 4 3 2 1
CM PA 14 0 9 8 7 6 5 4 3 2 1

Library and Archives Canada Cataloguing in Publication

Chantler, Scott, author, artist
    The king's dragon / Scott Chantler.

(Three thieves ; bk. 4)
ISBN 978-1-55453-778-5 (bound)   ISBN 978-1-55453-779-2 (pbk.)

    1. Graphic novels. I. Title. II. Series: Chantler, Scott.
Three thieves ; bk. 4.

PN6733.C53K56 2014   j741.5'971   C2013-905641-6

Kids Can Press is a /,©r\|s™ Entertainment company

THREE THIEVES
BOOK FOUR

The King's Dragon

SCOTT CHANTLER

Kids Can Press

ACT ONE

Knighted

CAPTAIN DRAKE, SIR?

HM?

MY APOLOGIES, SIR. I...I JUST ASKED IF YOU WERE ALL RIGHT.

WHY WOULDN'T I BE?

YOU SEEMED....

WELL.... YOU SEEMED FAR AWAY FOR A MOMENT.

I'M HERE, PHINEAS, AS YOU CAN PLAINLY SEE.

VERY WELL, THEN.

BUT IF IT'S SUCH A CLEAR CHOICE, WOULDN'T THEY *EXPECT* US TO LOOK HERE?

LIKELY. BUT THEY'RE DESPERATE.

ONE OF THEM'S HURT, AND BADLY.

SHE NEEDS A PLACE TO HEAL, ONE WHERE THEY WON'T GET CAUGHT. AND THE PODHU HEALERS TAKE AN OATH OF NEUTRALITY ON ALL MATTERS POLITICAL.

I'M GUESSING THEY'RE WILLING TO RISK DISCOVERY.

BUT ARE WE TOO LATE? ARE THEY *STILL* IN THERE, IS WHAT I'M ASKING.

IF THEY ARE, PHINEAS...

...I INTEND TO BRING THE PLACE DOWN AROUND THEIR EARS.

11

WELCOME, FRIENDS, TO THIS HOUSE OF HEALING.

HOW MAY WE BE OF SERVICE TO Y—?

WE'RE HERE BY ORDER OF HER MAJESTY, QUEEN MAGDA OF NORTH HUNTINGTON.

I HAVE REASON TO BELIEVE THAT YOU'RE SHELTERING THREE FUGITIVES WHO ESCAPED OUR CUSTODY.

FUGITIVES....?

A RED-HAIRED GIRL, A NORKER AND AN ETTIN WITH ONE HEAD, TRAVELING TOGETHER. YOU COULDN'T MISS THEM.

WHAT MAKES YOU THINK THAT THEY WOULD HAVE COME H—?

THE GIRL HAD A BROKEN LEG. NOW ARE THEY HERE OR AREN'T THEY?

I AM AFRAID I AM NOT AT LIBERTY TO SAY.

"NOT AT LIBERTY TO SAY"...?

WE PODHU ADMIT ALL WHO SEEK HEALING AND ENLIGHTENMENT.

IF WE SHOULD START ASSISTING IN THE CAPTURE OF THE FEW WHO COME TO US UNDER A CLOUD OF SIN, WE WOULD TURN AWAY THOSE WHO NEED US THE MOST.

AND WHAT IF WE COME IN AND TAKE A LOOK ANYWAY, HEALER? WHAT HAPPENS THEN?

CAPTAIN DRAKE, PLEASE....

IF YOU INSIST ON KILLING ME AND MY BROTHERS FOR THE SAKE OF QUARRY YOU ARE NOT EVEN CERTAIN LIES WITHIN...

15

...KNOW THAT YOU DO SO UNDER THE WATCHFUL EYE OF THE AVATAR, ON GROUND HE HAS DEEMED SACRED.

I...I'M SORRY.

WE ARE NOT IN NORTH HUNTINGTON, SIR! YOU AND YOUR FELLOW QUEEN'S DRAGONS HAVE NO AUTHORITY HERE!

THIS IS A HOUSE OF HEALING!

I WONDER WHO IT WAS... ORMYR? AND GRYLLUS, PERHAPS?

I'M LESS INTERESTED IN *WHO* THAN I AM IN *WHY...*

WHAT DO YOU MEAN?

DID VICTOR OF MEDORIA MENTION THAT HE'D SPOKEN TO ANY *OTHER* DRAGONS?

NO...

THEN HOW DID THEY KNOW TO LOOK HERE?

PERHAPS THEY HAVE RYUU WITH THEM. HE'S OUR BEST TRACKER...

PERHAPS.

YOU'RE YOUNG, PHINEAS, AND STILL EAGER TO SEE THE GOOD IN PEOPLE.

I'M GLAD FOR THAT. IT MEANS THEY HAVEN'T GOT TO YOU YET.

HAVEN'T POISONED YOUR MIND.

"THEY" WHO? WHAT DO YOU MEAN? THE DRAGONS...?

CAPTAIN...?

MY **ARM!** I-I THINK IT'S **BROKEN!**

YOU'LL GET WORSE THAN THAT FOR THREATENING THE LIFE OF THE KING!

TH-THREATENING HIM? I-I'VE TRIED TO **WARN** HIM!

"WARN HIM"---?

ABOUT THE IRON HAND! I'M NOT TRYING TO— I'M NOT ONE OF THEM! I-I'M **INNOCENT!**

KILL HIM!

FINISH THE JOB, DRAKE!

THIS MAN SAYS HE'S INNOCENT.

THEY **ALL** DO!

NOW **FINISH** IT!

ACT TWO

Tested

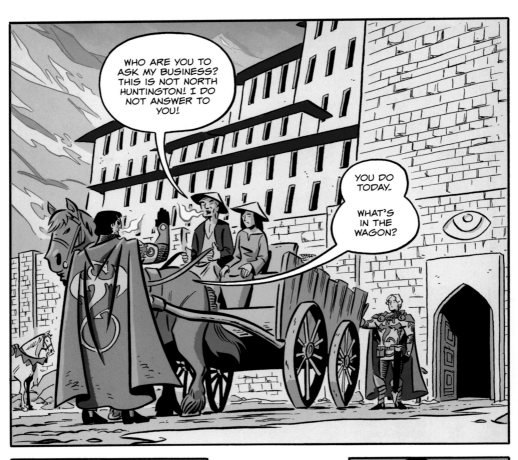

YOU REALLY THINK THEY'D HIDE IN A WAGON? THEY *MUST* KNOW WE'RE OUT HERE...

I DON'T PRETEND TO KNOW *WHAT* THESE REPROBATES WILL DO, PHINEAS.

YOU HAVE A BETTER IDEA?

NOT TO SECOND-GUESS YOU, CAPTAIN, BUT *ANYTHING* BEATS STANDING OUTSIDE WATCHING THE DOOR.

WHAT DID YOU SAY?

WE DON'T EVEN KNOW THEY'RE STILL *IN* THERE, IS WHAT I MEAN. UNTIL WE KNOW FOR SURE...

YOU'RE RIGHT.

I'LL GO IN AND SEE FOR MYSELF. AFTER NIGHTFALL, WHEN THE HEALERS ARE ASLEEP.

ALONE?

ALONE.

YOU'LL KEEP WATCH IN CASE THEY TRY TO MAKE THEIR ESCAPE WHILE I'M INSIDE.

VERY WELL.

BUSY MORNING FOR THE PODHU HEALERS....

INDEED.

HALT!

...I WON'T ASK AGAIN. NOW **WHERE IS IT?**

I ASSURE YOU, SIRE...

...THE LETT... HAS BEEN DESTROYED JUST AS YO... WISHED...

GOD'S TEETH, GREYFALCON! IF IT WAS TO BE DESTROYED, I'D HAVE SEEN TO IT MYSELF, TO BE—

TO BE CERTAIN IT REALLY **WAS?**

MAJESTY, I AM INJURED BY YOUR LACK OF TRUST.

YOU'LL BE INJURED BY THE **POINT OF MY SWORD** IF YOU DON'T WATCH YOUR STEP, CHAMBERLAIN.

ALL ALONE, DRAKE...?

YOU'RE ON GUARD ALL NIGHT. AND WITH GREYFALCON AND THE OTHER DRAGONS GONE, YOU COULD SEARCH HIGH AND LOW WITHOUT RISKING NOTICE.

IF THE LETTER STILL EXISTS, AS YOU SUSPECT, SIRE, IT WILL BE IN YOUR HANDS BEFORE SUNRISE.

I'D LIKE TO GET STARTED RIGHT AWAY.

I TRUST YOU, DRAKE. BUT IF YOU SHOULD FIND THE LETTER, PLEASE DON'T READ IT.

IT'S....

IT'S PERSONAL.

I SERVE THE THRONE OF NORTH HUNTINGTON, SIRE.

YOUR WILL IS MY COMMAND.

YOU LOOK LIKE YOU'VE SEEN A GHOST, DRAKE.

ONE OF THE HEALERS TOLD US THAT OTHERS HAD BEEN HERE. I SHOULD HAVE KNOWN IT WAS YOU.

HOW DID YOU—?

KNOW THE THREE THIEVES WERE HERE? I HAVE RYUU WITH ME.

PHINEAS SUSPECTED AS MUCH.

BROUGHT THE BOY, DID YOU?

HE'S AN *IDEALIST.* LIKE ANOTHER YOUNG RECRUIT I REMEMBER.

THE GIRL IS WOUNDED.

WE KNOW. ONLY TWO SETS OF TRACKS. SHE WAS CARRIED BY THE ETTIN.

THE PODHU AREN'T VERY TRUSTING. THEY WOULDN'T LET *US* IN, EITHER.

THEN LET'S HAVE A LOOK AROUND BEFORE WE'RE DISCOVERED.

GREYFALCON.

Astaroth

GONG

klack

WELCOME, FRIENDS, TO THIS HOUSE OF HE—

WHERE DID YOU GET THIS?

A MORE APPROPRIATE QUESTION, SIR KNIGHT, MIGHT BE WHERE DID *YOU* GET IT?

I'M IN NO MOOD FOR GAMES. *WHERE DID YOU GET IT?*

DRAKE....

...HOW DO YOU **KNOW** IT BELONGS TO GREYFALCON?

KNOW ANYONE **ELSE** WHO BUILDS MACHINES LIKE THE ONES IN HERE?

GREYFALCON...!

YOU KNOW HIM?

YES. A HARSH MAN.

IT **CAN'T** BE...

OUR THIEVES SHOW UP IN THE VERY SAME PLACE GREYFALCON DOES? **HERE**, OF ALL PLACES?

WHEN WAS HE HERE? AND WHY?

WAS HE HURT?

A WHILE AGO. THREE MOONS AT LEAST. AND NOT HURT.

HE WANTED TO SEE THE **PIGEONS.**

60

CARRIER PIGEONS, DRAKE?

GREYFALCON OFTEN RECEIVED THEM IN HIS CHAMBER. WHERE WERE THEY COMING FROM?

NEVER GAVE IT MUCH THOUGHT.

BECAUSE IT'S *NONE OF OUR CONCERN.*

THIS WAY, DRAGONS, THIS WAY.

STAND ASIDE, FRAYNIR.

THAT'S AN *ORDER.*

WE OF THE ORDER HAVE KEPT PIGEONS HERE FOR CENTURIES, ALLOWING MESSAGES TO BE CARRIED TO AND FROM ALL PARTS OF THE SIX KINGDOMS.

FROM HANBROOK TO THE SILVER COAST, FROM MAGISHEAD ALL THE WAY TO THE MOUNTAINS.

EVEN OUT TO SEA, AS FAR AS THE ISLAND OF ASTAROTH.

WITH ALL DUE RESPECT, CAPTAIN...

...EVEN IF THIS IS WHERE GREYFALCON'S PIGEONS CAME FROM, WHAT DOES THAT HAVE TO DO WITH WHETHER OUR THREE THIEVES WERE—?

WAIT.

THE ISLAND OF *WHAT?*

ACT THREE

Blinded

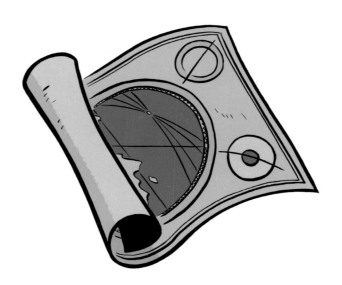

WE KNOW HOW CLEVER THESE THREE ARE. ONCE THEY'RE OUT OF THE SNOW, THEY'LL TRY TO DISGUISE THEIR TRACKS AS MUCH AS THEY CAN.

TOO BAD FOR THEM THAT RYUU COULD TRACK A FISH THROUGH WATER.

HOW *DID* YOU PICK UP THEIR TRAIL?

WHAT DO YOU MEAN? WE'VE BEEN FOLLOWING THEM SINCE KINGSBRIDGE, JUST AS YOU HAVE.

BUT THE TRAIL WENT COLD AT BLACK ROCK COVE. WHERE DID YOU PICK IT UP AGAIN?

IT'S CLEAR THEY'RE HEADING WEST. SO MEDORIA SEEMED AS GOOD A PLACE TO LOOK AS ANY.

YOU SEEM TO HAVE HAD THE SAME IDEA, AFTER ALL.

MEDORIA'S A BIG PLACE. YOU'RE TELLING ME YOU JUST HAPPENED UPON THEIR TRACKS?

THE AVATAR HIMSELF NEVER PRODUCED SUCH A MIRACLE.

WHAT ARE YOU GETTING AT, BOY?

IT'S *CAPTAIN.*

AND JUST HOW DID *YOU* END UP HERE, *"CAPTAIN"*?

WE HAD AN AUDIENCE WITH THE KING OF MEDORIA. HE HAD A RATHER...*DRAMATIC*... ENCOUNTER WITH OUR QUARRY LESS THAN TWO MOONS AGO.

WE DID THE SAME.

NO.

YOU DIDN'T.

KING VICTOR DIDN'T SAY A WORD ABOUT HAVING SEEN ANYONE ELSE OF OUR ORDER.

FATHER...?

GOD'S TEETH!

FATHER!

WHAT IS IT?

RYUU SAYS THE TRACKS DIVERGE HERE.

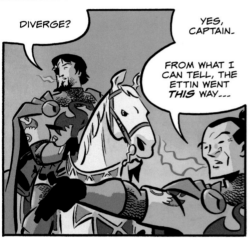

DIVERGE?

YES, CAPTAIN.

FROM WHAT I CAN TELL, THE ETTIN WENT *THIS* WAY...

...AND THE NORKER WENT *THAT* WAY.

ARE YOU SURE?

YES.

LOOK!

THERE'S EVEN A *CIGAR STUB* TO PROVE IT.

PFFT.

THEY'RE GETTING CARELESS. IT'S ALMOST LIKE THEY *WANT* TO BE FOLLOWED!

HAVE THEY EVER SPLIT UP BEFORE?

NOT THAT I KNOW OF. THEY'VE BEEN AS THICK AS...WELL, THIEVES.

LIKE THEY WANT TO BE FOLLOWED....

CAPTAIN...?

OF COURSE. THAT'S WHY I *MUST* GET YOU TO SAFETY.

ALL RIGHT.

BUT YOU'LL HAVE TO *CARRY* ME.

VERY WELL, MADAM.

TO THINK THAT GREYFALCON WANTS TO BUILD *TRAPS* IN THIS TOWER. THE STAIRS ALONE SEEM CHALLENGE ENOUGH!

<HUFF!> I HADN'T NOTICED.

79

BOOOM

Astaroth

KLUNK

...BUT THEY *DO* HAVE THEM.

Bump!

NO!

HEY!

<GASP!>

THE IRON HAND!

LIKE OUR DISGUISES?

MADE BY THE VERY SAME TAILOR YOU SILENCED FOR US, THAT SQUEALING RAT. WE OUGHT TO THANK YOU.

YOU CAN THANK ME FROM THE *GALLOWS*, ASSASSIN.

I DON'T THINK SO....

KEEP STILL! I'LL THROW YOU THE ROPE AND LIFT YOU BACK UP. BUT ONLY IF YOU SURRENDER TO ME AT THE TOP.

NEVER!

WILLFUL CHILD!

WHAT'S SO IMPORTANT ABOUT THAT WEATHER-BITTEN SEA CHART?

WHAT'S ON THIS ISLAND OF ASTAROTH?

MY BROTHER! I THINK...

SO YOU'RE NOT JUST RUNNING FROM US...

YOU'RE ALSO CHASING GREYFALCON...

HE KIDNAPPED MY BROTHER. AND YOU AND YOUR DRAGONS HELPED HIM DO IT!

I DON'T SERVE HIM. I SERVE THE THRONE.

AND THE QUEEN WANTS YOUR HEAD.

AND I WANT MY BROTHER BACK, YOU BLACK-HEARTED BULLY!

I CAN'T HELP YOU WITH THAT.

LET ME PULL YOU UP, AND I'LL ASK THE QUEEN TO BE LENIENT.

I'LL DIE FIRST!

YOU'RE BRAVE, GIRL, BUT NOT *THAT* BRAVE.

IF I HAVE TO CLIMB OUT THERE AND GET YOU, YOU'RE GOING TO BE A SORRY LITTLE—

HE'S LOST THE EYE, I'M AFRAID...

...AND THAT SCAR WILL NEVER FULLY HEAL.

BUT HE'LL LIVE. HOPEFULLY TO SERVE YOUR MAJESTY FOR MANY YEARS TO COME.

ON THIS MOST HORRIBLE OF EVENINGS, WE'VE AT LEAST THAT ONE BLESSING TO CLING TO.

THE ASSASSINS HAVE FLED?

JUMPED RIGHT FROM THE TOWER.

PERHAPS CHAMBERLAIN GREYFALCON'S PLAN TO BETTER SECURE THE TREASURY HAS MERIT AFTER ALL.

G...

HE STIRS, MADAM!

GR...

...AND THAT WAS WHEN SIR FRAYNIR SENT ME BACK FOR YOU.

THEY'VE CONTINUED ON AFTER THE ETTIN AND THE NORKER.

PERHAPS *THEY'LL* HAVE BETTER LUCK.

YOU'RE SURE YOU WON'T TAKE MY HORSE, CAPTAIN? I'D BE HAPPY TO WALK IN YOUR PLACE.

I'M NOT ENTITLED TO RIDE A HORSE, PHINEAS, HAVING LOST MINE.

THE QUEEN SHOULD TAKE MY SWORD AND CAPE, TOO, AND BE RID OF ME.

I'VE FAILED HIM.

AGAIN.

"HIM," SIR? YOU MEAN "HER." QUEEN MAGDA?

HM? YES. OF COURSE.

THE QUEEN.

WE'LL CATCH THAT GIRL, CAPTAIN, YOU'LL SEE. NOBODY MAKES FOOLS OF THE QUEEN'S DRAGONS.

WE'LL CHASE HER INTO THE SEA IF NEED BE.

109

INTO THE SEA...

I'VE *MISSED* SOMETHING, PHINEAS... SOMETHING *IMPORTANT*.

I CAN SWING A SWORD, AND FOLLOW ORDERS, AND *GIVE* THEM... BUT I HAVEN'T THE IMAGINATION FOR PUZZLES. NEVER DID.

THIS GIRL, THE BROTHER SHE TALKS ABOUT, ASTAROTH, GREYFALCON...IT'S A *PUZZLE*.

THERE'S *SOMETHING*, JUST BEYOND MY REACH.

I JUST CAN'T *SEE* IT...

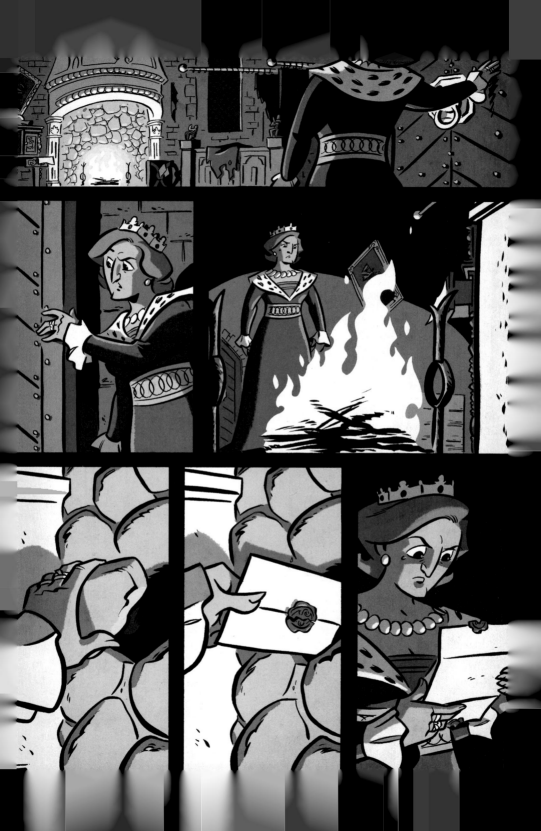